From Toxic to Tranquility:

How to claim your peace in a toxic work environment

Dr. Krisha Hawkins

From Toxic to Tranquility:
How to claim your peace in a toxic work
environment

From Toxic to Tranquility:
How to claim your peace in a toxic work
environment

Contents

A doctor, a patient, and a counselor.................5

Why don't YOU just leave?............................20

You are not alone...39

A grain of salt...50

System Errors..59

Options...66

Three C's..74

One Last Story 85

From Toxic to Tranquility:
How to claim your peace in a toxic work environment

A doctor, a patient, and a counselor

After running out to grab lunch, I pulled into a parking spot. Instead of getting out, I opted to sit in my car to eat. At the time, I didn't know why I chose that space to eat. It was almost like a survival instinct, something I did without thinking. I sat and felt oddly safe. Outside...in the car...in the parking lot, I felt safe but, in a weird way. At the same time, I felt strangely anxious. Admittingly, it is a strange dichotomy, to feel safe and anxious at the same time. In retrospect, I suppose it is odd, out of all the emotions, to consciously have a feeling of safety while sitting in a car and eating. Nevertheless, it is how I clearly remember feeling. I also remember that my car wasn't the most comfortable place to eat. As a matter of fact, I felt a strange ache in my lower back. Dismissing the ache as a symptom of sleeping in an awkward position the night before, I stayed in my safe space to enjoy my lunch.

Sitting in front of my steering wheel, the bottled water sat in my cup holder. I had wrapped a napkin around the plastic in an attempt to absorb the condensation from the cold bottle. The plastic bag, that held my lunch, sat neatly in my lap. In my safe place, I attempted to open my small ranch dipping sauce tray. After an unsuccessful attempt to pull the ranch foil open by prying the corner of the packet with my fingertip, I became irritated. Once opened, half of the ranch sauce spilled onto the foam plate.

Skipping the sauce in the package, I dipped my chicken strip into the wasted sauce from the plate and took a bite. I immediately noticed the tightness in my jaws. For some reason, eating was difficult, almost impossible. As much as I tried to chew, my jaws seemed either unwilling or unable to participate in the rhythmic, mechanical, and normally instantaneous action. Being clinically minded, I mentally grappled with the cause of my current inability to do something so simple! I sat still and began to critically think about my predicament while simultaneously assuming the roles of my own doctor, patient, and counselor. "Girl! Are you having a stroke?" I silently questioned myself. I felt the tightness radiate from my jaw to my neck. Again, in my head, the group of three began to counsel me but, this time with a scolding tone, "Wait a minute! You cannot be having a heart attack!" Like the way one would warm up prior to exercise, I slowly attempted to move my chin forward, so it could touch my chest. I felt my shoulder muscles twitch, almost shiver as if I were in the cold. The faint back pain that I experienced earlier had now intensified. Looking at my reflection in my rearview mirror, I examined myself for any noticeable facial droop that might indicate a sign of a stroke. Seeing none, I continued with my self-assessment by moving my lips, my mouth still holding the unchewed chicken strip, in a slow upward turn to attempt to smile. The look was far from attractive, but my fake and forced smile showed facial evenness on both sides. It was during this random act, of getting my lunch and trying to eat that I had to face the reality that something was terribly wrong.

To be completely honest with myself, I was never consistently good at recognizing and addressing my own stress. Happiness, of course, was easy. I could even realize when I was angry. But, stress was a tough one. In my opinion, crying or lamenting about life's challenges was a time waster. What will I do when I finished crying (my inner counselor voice would ask)? I would reason with myself by saying, after the tears, the issue or problem would yet remain and had to be addressed. Consequently, my inner counselor would assist me in concluding that there was no time to tackle the issue like the present. So, I saved the tears and allocated my time to prayer and strategic problem-solving. To put this into context, tears during a sad movie, world events or something that happened in someone else's life were acceptable. But, crying or worrying about my own life issues, no way! Before you judge me, please let me do the honors. I.WAS.A.MESS!

I suppose, at some time in my life, I developed this practice of shrugging off stress as a coping mechanism. Who knows? What I did know for sure was that I was sitting in my car, with an unchewed chicken strip in my mouth, an awful backache, neck pain, and a feeling of safe anxiety. What does that even mean?

In retrospect, I now believe that my sense of safety was related to my sense of "being away". My sense of anxiety was related to my feeling of "having to go back". I hated the mere thought of going back to work. When away, I felt I could breathe if only until the next workday, or in this case until my lunch break was over. I felt unappreciated by the organization and that my current supervisor's behavior contributed to a toxic work environment. What's more, I believed the work environment or culture ignored or at times, even rewarded the toxic behavior. Although I was in touch with those feelings, I was out of touch with how it was affecting me. Up until then, I was certain that I was effectively coping. Sitting in my car that day, my body demonstrated the feelings that I refused to acknowledge. Paralyzed and panicked by the thought of going back to work, I came face to face with some hard truths about my situation. Chewing a chicken strip was taking the same jaw effort that one would use when trying to chew an old, frozen piece of children's bubble gum. Lowering my chin to my chest made me feel as if I were pushing a boulder uphill. These simple tasks suddenly seemed impossible and tired me to my core. The stress from my job and the organizational culture were making me physically sick.

In an environment where my pay was reasonable, and I actually loved the work that I was hired to do why did it feel as if this job, or to be totally honest, working for this manager was making me sick? Can you recall a time being in a similar situation? Are you experiencing these feelings right now? Can you relate? Are your feelings related to a supervisor or manager? Perhaps, your feelings are related to an organizational structure, a workplace climate, or a system? If you find yourself in this situation, then this book is for you. I want to encourage you and let you know that you can get through this!

When faced with my situation, I want to be completely honest with you. I was not perfect. As a matter of fact, as you can see from my ineffective coping mechanisms, I made some costly mistakes. I want to encourage you and share some perspectives that I've learned. However, before we move ahead, I need to be transparent with you.

• This book will not tell you how to deal with a tough boss. While a toxic manager can also be tough, a tough boss (one with high expectations) is not necessarily toxic. High employee expectations are not necessarily negative. In contrast, when employees are provided with clear expectations and the appropriate resources to perform, high expectations can often be a motivator to high-performing employees.

• This book will not tell you ways to avoid accountability. This is somewhat related to the first bullet. If, for some reason, you have been provided with the tools to do your work, but you are not performing in a satisfactory manner (for example, coming to work late, taking excessive breaks, completing poor quality work, exhibiting a poor attitude that has been consistent throughout your life), this book will not attempt to excuse or condone those behaviors.

• Lastly, this book will not tell you how to get revenge on your boss, your company, or your chosen profession (Darn it!). This is not a revenge book or a way to help you overthrow the establishment in your office. As satisfying as the thought may be to see your boss being escorted out of the premises with his/her belongings in a cardboard box, this book will not focus on "101 ways to get your boss fired". Sorry!

But…keep reading! Stay with me. Although you may have a "toxic" boss today, that boss may get another job, lose his/her current job, or retire. You may work for a toxic organization today. However, companies restructure, top leadership changes, and the organizational culture may shift. You may even work in a seemingly thankless profession where the rules, regulations, structures, and guidelines create a "lose/lose" scenario for the people you try to serve and those who serve. People (even toxic bosses) change jobs. Organizations change focus and professions institute new guidelines. In all of those scenarios, the constant or element that is consistent is you! See, even if you pray that boss away, he/she may be replaced by another one. If you change places of employment, you may be faced with an organizational system of structure that is not easy to thrive in. You can even change professions and run into similar lose/lose scenarios. Yikes!

So, instead of focusing on things that may be transient in your life, this book will focus on you! In this book, I will share stories of others who have experienced some of the same things you may be experiencing. We will reflect on our feelings and create actionable steps. This book will provide you with tools to help you through your situation. Finally, it is my prayer that this book will provide you with a place to heal.

Questions for reflection:

1.   Do you feel that you are in tune with your feelings of stress?

2.   How do you handle workplace stress? Do you have outbursts with customers or with other co-workers?

3.   What personal strategies have you employed to deal with your situation?

4.   If you believe that your boss is contributing to our unhealthy work environment, do you feel that him/her leaving the organization will completely solve your problem? Why or why not?

Why don't YOU just leave?

So, why did I stay? Why didn't I just pack my own belongings in a cardboard box, salvage my peace, and take the voice that I felt was unvalued or ignored, and take my talents elsewhere? Feeling helpless to change the situation and unwilling to walk away from the job, I determined that I would simply tough it out. I met my deadlines and pressed to ensure my work exhibited a satisfactory level of quality. When necessary, I made the appropriate eye contact to appear concerned. After failed attempts to discuss my concerns, I made it a point to purposefully withhold outward emotion or facial expressions. In my view, showing emotion, in my current environment was akin to showing weakness. With each toxic maneuver that my boss imposed, I determined I would employ a "rope-a-dope" strategy by taking the "punches" and letting the situation tire itself out. Unfortunately, I was the one that was exhausted.

After all, I often rationalized with myself, "I'm blessed to have a job. Although I won't make the Forbes list of the richest people by working here, there are certainly those who are less well off." It will be okay. Being an African-American woman, I even thought about the stories related to slavery and the Civil Rights era. I determined that "if they could endure all that they went through and succeed, So.Can.I". Yes, I am ashamed to say, my ineffective, ill-trained and inner counselor even brought my ancestors into this mess. I felt as if my coping skills were sufficient. When faced with high stress in a high-stakes environment, given the instinctual choice of fight or flight, I decided to stay. Disengagement was my way of surviving. Right or wrong, it was my way of fighting. I thought I was okay and felt this was an acceptable, safe, and justified way to manage my predicament.

If I were to describe my disengagement, I would say it was a slow and progressive process. I did not blow up with a customer or yell at work. However, I stopped offering suggestions to fix issues. I stopped being creative and simply "colored within the lines". Whether it was sick leave, vacation time, or unscheduled "emergencies", I started taking more time off and left work as soon as it was time to go…Not.One.Second.Later. I am sure, some who are reading this will say I was exhibiting passive-aggressive behavior. At times, I am sure this is true. I felt I had lost my voice in this workplace and no longer felt valued. The distinction is that I knew I had value to offer.

So, I started this chapter off by sharing some of the reasons that I stayed. I guess the bigger question would be, why do people stay in any toxic relationship? As odd as it may appear, some of the reasons that people remain in toxic workplace cultures are similar to the reasons that people stay in toxic relationships. After all, unless you work in a virtual environment from home or you work in a family business, most employees spend more time with their co-workers than with their family members. As a matter of fact, the term "work family" has real credibility for many. It is not uncommon to share pictures of milestone events such as a graduation, wedding, or from the birth of a new child. As much as some may want or feel the need to keep a clear separation between work and personal, there will always be aspects where the two are crossed. So, why do people stay in unhealthy work environments? While this list is certainly not exhaustive, I would like to explore a couple of reasons with you.

Depending on the reason you chose to work in your organization or profession, you may feel a strong connection to the mission. Chances are, if you feel the work that you are doing is tied to a purpose that is bigger than you, then you may work to remain in an unhealthy work environment despite your personal feelings of stress or discontentment. Leaving the organization could be perceived as abandoning the mission.

There are good reasons why companies take the time to fine-tune their vision and mission statements and ensure they are communicated to employees. Of course, one of those reasons is that organizations want their customers to know what the company believes in. However, another and perhaps equally important reason is related to building a connection with the employees. In most cases, the mission focuses on the strategy while the vision focuses on the future. Chances are, if you feel a strong connection or purpose that is aligned with your organizational mission and you can identify with your role in helping achieve the company's goals, then you may find leaving an unhealthy work environment to be difficult.

To add insult to injury, these strong connections may make it harder to work in an unhealthy work environment as you may perceive that the current organizational structure, policies, or leadership style puts the mission and vision in jeopardy. I need to make a distinction between two mindsets. One mindset says that you are connected to or feel a strong sense of the mission and see yourself as a part of the vision as a sense of purpose. Another mindset says that you are connected to or feel a strong sense of the mission and see yourself as a part of the vision because no one can do the work that you are doing as good as you can or no one else can be as passionate about the work as you are. The first mindset is, on its merits, about service. It centers on your connection, desire, and purpose to serve. It can drive you to struggle to remain focused on the work despite the circumstances. The second mindset, on its merits, is about self-gratification. Staying in a toxic work environment, in this case, can be more about fulfilling an internal feeling of insecurity. In other words, it can be an effort to show just how indispensable or worthy you believe you are. In either case, without a supportive and healthy work environment, it can be extremely difficult to excel.

Another reason that some people stay in unhealthy work environments is that they feel a sense of entrapment by their circumstances. Similar to the way some people stay years in an unhealthy marriage and justify it by saying they are staying because they don't want to split their financial assets, people have financial capital connected to their place of employment. Perhaps you are vested in a retirement plan that you do not want to (or do not feel you can financially afford to) walk away from. There may be hope for a promotion or an opportunity to change departments that you do not want to lose. Without regard to the organizational mission and vision statement, your sense of obligation to your own personal mission to survive and vision to have your bills paid in the future may stir feelings of fear and entrapment. Survival is indeed an instinct and if you have tied your ability to survive to your workplace, then it will be difficult to see yourself walking away- even when your health (mental or physical) is negatively impacted.

A third reason that people feel compelled to stay in an unhealthy work environment is that they feel they are there to positively influence or change the culture. I have found that this belief does not have to be directly tied to positional authority. Sometimes, those with informal authority have the power to influence the most. Do you know of a janitor who whistles or sings while working and whose presence seems to brighten up the halls? Perhaps that person is a hospital unit clerk or nursing assistant who manages to make everything seem calm when all hell is breaking loose. If you are in a position of formal authority, you may feel the sense to stay to protect or mitigate the impact of an unhealthy work environment to your subordinates. If you are in middle management, it is possible that you find yourself in a strange conflict where subordinates may erroneously perceive that you have the power to influence or communicate change at levels that you may not actually have. Acting as the middle person who is "stuck" between the employees and the leadership authority can serve as a conduit of stress all by itself. On the other hand, you may find yourself at a higher leadership level within your organization. While it may seem as if someone in this position could easily make changes, this is not always true. Those who at higher levels of authority may feel helpless to influence change if they are under the constraints of an ill-written policy or some other law. Whatever organizational position of authority (informal or formal) someone may find themselves in, if you feel responsible for or believe you are able to make a positive influence on others, you may stay in an unhealthy environment even to the detriment of your own personal health. In these cases, leaving may even lead to a feeling of being disloyal or abandonment to those who may be "left behind".

The final reason that I would like to explore with you is simple, but perhaps the most complex. As humans, most of us simply do not like disruptive change. Sometimes when given the opportunity to change and face the unknown, we will stay in our present state of pain and nurse that unhealthy area in hopes that it will either heal or at the least that we can become numb to it. As a young girl, my daughter had long, thick, and gorgeous hair. I remember how I would twirl her hair around my index finger and assemble the most beautiful head of ringlet curls. As she got older, she got more active in sports. The perspiration and consistent high ponytails resulted in unhealthy hair. Clearly, I could see that her hair was damaged and unhealthy. When looking at her style her hair one day, I suggested that she go and get a haircut. I explained, as motherly as I could, that this was necessary to allow the healthy hair to start growing again. Although my daughter remembered the past state of her hair and saw the current state of her hair, she vehemently refused to get a haircut. In her eyes, she would rather keep the long and unhealthy hair than to deal with the change and transition that came along with a cut. She was used to having long hair and remembered the past compliments as people adored her thick, long, index finger-rolled curls. However now, when faced with the decision to change, she was unwilling to see herself differently and had, in fact, attached a part of her identity to being "the girl with the thick, long hair". Finally, after my insistence, my daughter reluctantly got her haircut. When she returned home she went straight to her room and closed the door. Curious and concerned, I went to her room and found her sitting on her bed in disgust. With tears in her eyes, a pout, and a voice of exasperation and defeat, she looked at me and said, "I look like Lord Farquaad from Shrek." As much as I wanted to dispute her self-assessment, the truth was that she did! Knowing that it was not the appropriate time to joke about such a "serious" matter, I simply told her that she could find another stylist to shape it better. Well, she did find another stylist and her hair quickly started to regain its healthy shine and length. Today, she is a little too old for the finger ringlets, but, her hair is in great shape.

For similar reasons, we often fear change. Even when we know that remaining in our current situation is damaging us or is unhealthy, we often chose to stay because we have become accustomed to the identity that comes along with working for a particular company, being in a particular profession, or holding a certain position. Let's face it, even when we muster the strength to make a change, it doesn't feel good at first. We may be in a "Lord Farquad" phase until we regain our footing. Change can be hard and scary. While some seem to wistfully flow through life, most of us have a hard time with an unplanned change that feels forced upon us. Planned and chosen change is one thing but, disruptive change that feels out of our control can be intimidating.

As you read through some of the reasons that people stay in unhealthy work environments, did any resonate with you? It's okay if they did. This is certainly a no judgment zone. Remember, I shared my experience and behavior in working in an unhealthy work environment and I did not always do the right thing either. The body and mind can do strange things when faced with a fight or flight decision. Take a moment to reflect on your behavior and the subconscious reasons that you may have given yourself to justify staying or going.

Questions for reflection:

1.   What does "disengagement" look like in your current work environment? Have you become disengaged at work?

2. Do you feel a strong connection to your organizational mission and vision? If so, do you think this connection is based on a desire to serve or is it based on self-gratification? Do you feel that either of these desires are strong enough for you to stay in your current environment?

3. If you had an opportunity to leave your current organization or department for an opportunity that offered slightly

less pay, would you do it? If no, why not? How would you survive if your company went out of business or had a massive layoff that impacted you?

4. Outside of the work environment, how do you handle disruptive change? Do you see any differences or similarities in the way you manage change at work?

You are not alone

Now that we have explored some of the reasons that people remain in unhealthy work environments, I would like for us to take some time to take a deeper dive and look at the impact that this decision can have on you. Unfortunately, our experiences are not isolated. There's an old saying about being "a fly on the wall". It is presumed, that in this position a person is unassuming and therefore able to hear and see whatever occurs in a genuine (without pretense) environment. Oh boy! If you could only be a fly on the wall behind some of the closed office doors where people congregate and whisper, during "happy" hour at the local bar, or at some of your colleague's homes, you would quickly understand that there a lot of people who find themselves in this predicament.

According to a recent Gallup World poll, a dismal 15 percent of "the world's one billion full-time workers are engaged at work " (GALLUP, INC). When looking at working-age adults across 155 countries, Gallup found that the number of employees who were "highly involved in and enthusiastic about their work and workplace" was an unimpressive 15 percent. In the United States, Gallup's 2017 report shows a more promising picture. Out of over 100 million full-time employees in the American workforce, about 33 percent feel that they are in a promising and engaging environment. Approximately 16 percent report being "actively disengaged" meaning they are miserable. The remaining 51 percent is not "engaged at all". In other words, they are just there to collect the check and go home.

When we look at other studies that focus on various professions, it's is not overwhelmingly encouraging. In a study of over 95,000 nurses in the United States, 24 percent who provide care to patients at the bedside and 27 percent who provide care to patients in nursing homes report being dissatisfied and frustrated. A different study looked at burnout and dissatisfaction among 300 physicians. Ninety-six percent say they have either witnessed or experienced negative impacts as a result of burnout or dissatisfaction. A Gallup poll that focused on the condition of schools in the United States revealed that 7 out of

10 teachers report not feeling emotionally connected to or dissatisfied with their workplaces. This is just three professional groups where dissatisfaction or burnout is at alarming rates.

Another data research company reveals that 77 percent of employees experience physical symptoms of stress caused by bad bosses. Symptoms such as moodiness, feelings of a loss of control or powerlessness, forgetfulness, an inability to relax, chest pain, insomnia, rapid heartbeat, and headaches are the most commonly reported. Additionally, employees with ineffective managers have been found to be 60 percent more likely to suffer from heart trauma and 30 percent more likely to suffer from coronary heart disease.

I had a co-worker who I will call "John". In addition to his full-time job, John was a pastor at a local church. At one point in his career, he was upbeat and talked about enjoying his work and being at the company. Other employees often went to John to work on extra tasks because of his positive attitude and work ethic. However, his department underwent leadership changes and John was feeling bullied by his current supervisor. In John's perspective, he went from being an outstanding employee to where he now felt he couldn't "do anything right". When John sought constructive feedback from his supervisor, it got worse. Instead of receiving positive feedback for improvement, the supervisor took the opportunity to further degrade him by telling him that he was on "thin ice" and scolding him about sharing his ideas during the last staff meeting. After a little over a year of this treatment, John (the once-upbeat employee) shared that he wanted to quit. However, he feared that he could not find a similar job with comparable pay. John had a family who was depending on him and a young church that he was not financially stable enough to give him a full salary. This was not just a psychological decision, it was a financial decision and John felt trapped.

However, the breaking point came when one of the members John's church called him in the middle of the night. The member shared that her ailing husband had died after a lengthy battle with a terminal illness. While John's wife immediately began to console the grieving widow, John admitted to feeling frozen. He said he was genuinely sad about the death of his church member and the grief that the family was in. However, he stated that he simply could not muster the strength to console. As a matter of fact, John reported that, outside of work, he no longer had the energy to do much these days. It was apparent that going to work and trying to function and survive was taking all of John's emotional and physical energy. Slowly, John went into a fight or flight mode where his survival instincts went into gear. Now, even the things that John normally enjoyed like family, church, and friends required too much energy.

I hope we can safely assume that John felt a strong connection to the mission of being a pastor. To some, it may sound horrible for a pastor to be unable to function at a time when a member needs him/her the most. However, extended exposure to a psychologically unhealthy working environment has the potential to negatively impact even the strongest sense of responsibility. One lady, who once shared her story with me was once a strong volunteer and contributor on her daughter's parent-teacher association. However, now she found herself no longer able to volunteer. She simply wanted to go home, rest, and get prepared for the next work day.

I've shared my story and my experience. I also shared John's story. What is your story?

Questions for reflection:

1)   Does simply going to work take all your emotional energy to the point that you have nothing left when you get home?

2)   Has your family or friends noticed a change in your behavior? Have you experienced any of the physical symptoms of stress that you believe are influenced by your workplace environment?

3)   Do you have an inner and ill-trained counselor who is denying the real physical and/or mental health impact that your unhealthy workplace is having on you?

If you answered yes to any of those questions, and you have not done so already, I encourage you to reach out to someone you trust. Start the conversation about how your experience is impacting you.

• The National Suicide Prevention Hotline is a free and confidential support service that is available to anyone who is in emotional distress. The hotline is available 24 hours a day and 7 days a week and can be assessed by phone at 1-800-273-8255. Additionally, the website is as follows: http://suicidepreventionlifeline.org/

• The Mental Health of America has a free depression screening with relevant resources. The website is as follows: http://www.mentalhealthamerica.net/depres sion-support-and-advocacy .

A grain of salt

I know! I know! I know!

I know I said, we are not going to focus on your supervisor, organization, or possible systemic (i.e., rules, regulations, governmental) processes that can lead to an unhealthy working environment. Well, we won't focus on it but, we have to talk about it. Positive and healthy work environments have positive impacts on employee health, organizational culture, and outcomes. Alternatively, negative and unhealthy work environments have negative impacts on employee health. Plus, as much as some of us may hate to admit it, "venting" (don't you think that sounds so much more positive than "complaining") can be therapeutic!

I can recall complaining to my friend about my supervisor saying that she "Has a heart the size of a grain of salt". Seemingly, decisions were made without reflection of the impact that they had on others. At times, it even appeared that decisions were made without reflection of the larger organizational impact. It appeared, at least from many of our vantage points, that her decision-making matrix was based on her needs. As long as the idea was phrased in a way that she believed she could take the credit, she supported it. However, if an idea gave others the opportunity to grow, then she discouraged or flat out denied it. I want to be clear, there were some employees who thrived under this supervisor. The supervisor appeared to enjoy working with those employees as evidenced by their after-hours meetings to go out to dinner or hang out. Not only did those employees call the supervisor by her first name, but they also called her husband by his first name and laughed about something funny that her children (who were also called by their first names) did. These employees never had a "bad" idea or request that wasn't hastily approved.

However, for the rest of us on the "iddy biddy committee", ideas and requests were voiced with trepidation. Out of fear of being made to feel guilty about the organizational needs, some staff were afraid to ask for time off to address personal obligations such as caring for an ailing parent. One employee experienced a catastrophic life event that caused her to be out of work for several days. I can remember her sharing that on her first day back to work, the supervisor immediately started asking her work-related questions without offering any type of condolences. On another occasion, another employee needed to unexpectedly leave work to take care of a sick child, the supervisor "asked" her to make sure she had tied up all of her loose ends up first and not to leave anything undone. The heart the size of a grain of salt!

I am sure that there are some cases where people's behavior is just nasty with no apparent reason. However, when we consider the way people are promoted in most roles, it has little to do with their ability to lead. In most cases, promotion comes with the ability to do the work at the next lowest (not higher) level. A person with technical expertise performs well so, he or she is promoted. Often, leadership training only occurs at the point in which the person is formally selected for the leadership position. The saying about "what got you to the top will keep you there" isn't completely true. Each level requires a new or expanded skill set.

The phrase "soft skills" has been given to the set of skills or characteristics that focus on a person's interpersonal (people) skills. Skills that typically fall into this category include communication, the ability to work in teams, emotional intelligence, conflict resolution, and motivation. With little to no exception, all jobs require some degree of soft skills. However, as people gain leadership positions of authority, the need for those skills become more critical. Unfortunately, many organizations do not place a high priority on a person's actual ability to lead until they are actually in a formal leadership role.

On the other hand, "hard skills" are the technical or measurable skills that are specifically required. If asked to create a resume, the hard skills would be easily identifiable and measurable. Unfortunately, being amazing at those measurable skills does not always equate to being competent at leadership. So, if your supervisor is the cause of your unhealthy work environment, it may not be the size of his heart at all. It may simply be related to your supervisor being untrained and unprepared to lead at the next level. Although this explanation does little to change the way you are being treated, it may help you to understand why you are experiencing this treatment. In the words of my grandmother, "He just doesn't know any better!"

If your boss's behavior is the result of poor or absent leadership training, I wish I could recommend one class that would be beneficial to immediately help. While I am an advocate of leadership training, people often forget that it is a form of development. In other words, don't expect your supervisor to go to one course or even a group of courses and immediately transform into a kind and effective leader. Development takes time and leadership development is both a process and a journey. That's one of the reasons why it is somewhat pointless to focus all of your energy on your supervisor in an unhealthy work environment. Remember, in chapter two we talked about how hard change and transition can be. This is true for your supervisor as well. It is probable that he/she does not even recognize the negative impact of her behavior. If they do recognize their behavior, it is equally possible that they have not yet figured out HOW to change.

Questions for reflection:

1.   How are people promoted within your organization? To your knowledge, are they promoted based on their ability to perform the technical work "hard

skills" or is there an emphasis on "soft skills"?

2.   I said my supervisor had "a heart the size of a grain of salt". What (if any) story have you said about your supervisor? Do you believe this actually reflects that person's character?

System Errors

W. Edwards Deming, a widely known business consultant, said, "A bad system will beat a good person every time". It is highly possible that you either like or at least have a neutral relationship with your boss and you still find yourself in an unhealthy workplace. For someone who feels a connection to an organizational mission or just wants to excel at work, nothing can be more frustrating than to be forced to work within an ineffective system.

In the healthcare system, physicians and nurses have communicated their angst about working within a system that they do not feel always puts the patient first. School teachers have spoken out about the constraints on their ability to exercise creativity in the current educational systems. Government employees have complained about bureaucratic systems that seem to impede change. It is highly probable that somewhere, in the midst of most of these issues, a person or group of people holds the answer to the business problem but, they don't feel as if they can change the system.

A friend of mines, who moved out of state, sent me a text one night. She simply said, "Call me when you can. I am getting discouraged and I need some encouragement." Immediately, I called her. She is an intelligent person who is extremely accomplished in her field of work. Although she was initially excited about her new job, she had become frustrated with her boss's response to her ideas. Her boss did not feel that her ideas were bad. He just didn't want to exert the organizational energy on implementing them.

Every day, my friend came home feeling exhausted and defeated from working in an area that she felt passionate about but helpless to enact real change. As she talked with me and shared her proposal to solve the organizational problem, it was almost as if I were in a briefing room with her. In her voice, I could hear the energy, enthusiasm, and passion about the circumstance. "If only he would give it a chance," she voiced, "I know this will work." After asking her questions to help explore her options, she weighed the pros, cons, and consequences of each one. If she stayed in her current circumstance, she feared becoming disengaged and unchallenged. If she approached her supervisor again, she feared he may take it as a waste of time, not listen again, and become frustrated with her. If she shared it with the next level of supervision, she feared retaliation. In a defeated tone, my friend expressed regret about her acceptance of a position that she was once excited about Slowly, she began to feel unappreciated, unheard, and hopeless to impact remarkable change. At the end of the conversation and after responding to my probing questions, my friend asked me to be her accountability partner. She was putting a plan together to start her own company and leave her current place of employment.

Questions for reflection:

1)   Think about the last two meaningful changes that occurred in your workplace. Were they a result of an idea that generated from leadership (above your level in the organization) or were the ideas generated from someone at your level or below?

2)   Think back on how you felt when you first started working at your place of employment or within your profession. What are some of the things that excited you about being there? How often (daily, once a week, once a month, yearly,

never) do you still feel at least half as excited as you did then?

3)   Do you feel "stuck" in an organization or organizational system that impedes your ability to impact change? Do you feel that you have explored all of your options? Are you still exploring options, or have you just decided to accept that change is too hard to implement? If you are no longer exploring options, how does this make you feel (disengaged or apathetic, feeling that you are not really making an impact, exhausted, angry, ready to quit).

4)   Do you ever feel compelled to start your own company? If so, what barriers (i.e., finances, fear) are stopping you from exploring that option? What plan of action can you put in place to address those challenges?

Options

With the exception of drinking my water, I didn't try to eat the rest of my lunch. After the pathetic attempt to eat my first chicken strip, I didn't have much of an appetite. In all honesty, I was afraid. A person can be in denial for a long time but, once you see and recognize the truth for what it is, it is difficult to un-see it. I reached out to a friend who I could talk this through with. In the past, I had complained about my situation before (remember my characterization of the size of my supervisor's heart). However, this conversation was not centered around the work environment or the boss. It was focused on me. "I have got to do something different", I remember telling her. Prior to that, I was feeling as if something different (I'm not sure what) would occur. Maybe my boss would get a new job and then, we can all breathe again. Maybe the company will finally do something about our complaints and hold her accountable (code word for security escort with a cardboard box). Maybe I could just go numb and act as if this was not happening or that it didn't matter. Maybe this and maybe that. Maybe never happened.

If I found a new job, I may encounter another unhealthy work environment. What would I do if I found myself in another dysfunctional organizational system? Maybe I am a bit of a pessimist but, I believed this was an area of my life that I felt I could not run away from and had to face head-on. I wanted to work through this so, I never again would allow anyone or any system to negatively impact me in this manner. The only certainty that I had was in my actions and even then, I knew that change would be difficult.

I've read and heard where people encouraged those in similar situations to "change your outlook". In other words, to start thinking about and focusing on the positive aspects of your situation. This advice would be doled out with all the simplicity of telling someone to change their shirt because it didn't match their shoes. While having a positive perspective is beneficial, the way that one consistently gets to that point is not always so simple. For some, I assume it is as simple as waking up and declaring that you have a positive outlook.

However, for the majority of us, it is not that easy.

I must admit, for a while, I felt ashamed that I was not able to consistently retain a positive mindset about my circumstance. As a matter of fact, I believed it to be a reflection of the condition of my spiritual relationship. Consequently, I was privately embarrassed when I would lose focus and end up either sulking, disengaging, or trying to ignore my situation again. If I must brag on myself, I would do amazing for about a week. However, after a sequence of negative occurrences with my supervisor (they didn't even have to be all my own personal occurrences) I would find myself recoiling in that same "unsafe" space where I had anxiety and no energy when I got home.

At the end of the day, our body has two main ways of dealing with stress (fight or flight (run away)). As insane as it sounds, I was fighting and running at the same time. It's no wonder why I was stressed! Even if I left the organization, I made up my mind that I was going to fight but for the right reason. I was no longer fighting to see my supervisor be brought to my perspective of justice (insert the image of security and a cardboard box again). I wasn't even fighting for organizational change. Without regard to my choice to stay or go, I was fighting for my peace and happiness. Beyond the pay, the benefits, and even the organizational mission, I did a real inventory of something that I could take with me wherever I went, and that was my peace and health. The truth is that all along, I had more options than what I focused on. No matter where you are in your organization and what educational degree you may and may not have, you have options too. I will repeat what I said earlier...once you see and acknowledge the truth, it is hard to un-see it. You may feel stuck in a hopeless situation, but you are not stuck!

In the end, I did leave. It was an exhilarating experience. I actually loved the work that I was doing but, it was time to go. This time when I left, I felt safe. I'm talking about a real sense of safety, not like an anxious sense of safety that I felt that day in my car. It was a feeling of safety and peace that I owned and not just rented during lunch or on the weekend. In the next chapter, I want to share some practical tips that I used to take me on my journey. Before I do, I have one last set of questions for you.

Questions for reflection:

1)　Do you have any truths about your situation that you cannot now un-see? Think about the conversations you have either had with others or with yourself about your situation? Have those conversations focused on your supervisor, your problem, or you?

2)   What ways have you tried to change your outlook or perspective about your situation? Can you think of any reasons why those attempts did not consistently last?

3)   If your supervisor never leaves and/or your organizational systems never change, aside from winning the lottery, what would a successful outcome of your situation look like to you?

From Toxic to Tranquility:
How to claim your peace in a toxic work environment

Three C's

At this point, you may have decided to stay and fight or you may have decided that leaving is best for you. The truth is, only you can make that decision for you. It is both my hope and prayer that you are able to come to a place of peace and health in whatever choice that you make. When I was in my situation, I didn't know what I was going to do. So, I used three main steps that I felt would apply to either choice: fight or flight. Throughout your and my time together, as we have shared stories and reflected. In some cases, we walked through these steps. For simplicity, I have named the steps the "Three C's": *Chart, Challenge, and Change*.

Chart:

As I shared in the at the beginning of the book, I realized that I was not the best at assessing my own stress levels. My inner and ill-trained counselor had good motives but, she had issues too. I desperately needed a way to check myself. While I had friends who I could call, I didn't want to depend on my ability to reach out or their availability every time I had an issue. I also had a prayer life, as a matter of fact, most days I had to pray just to get walk in the building. However, I would find myself losing focus in my prayerful conversations. If you are spiritual and have never found yourself in this predicament then, I applaud you but, I'm just not that impressive. While I know that God always knows and understands my heart and needs, I am sometimes confused.

In addition to my prayer conversations and wise counsel with friends, I desired a way to face my situation that would not leave me feeling defeated. I have a background in nursing and in healthcare, there is an old saying, "If it isn't charted then, it wasn't done." After everything is said and done, people often have a hard time remembering what actually occurred. Charting is an objective and historical method of documenting what happened with a patient encounter. For my workplace situation, with the exception of being objective, I employed a similar strategy through charting or the more commonly used term, journaling. As simple as it sounds, this was my first step towards peace. When writing, I could genuinely be myself and share my feelings without judgment. Even if it meant jotting a little down during my lunchtime, without regard to any consideration of what my ill-trained counselor would say, I was able to describe my experiences in all of their rawness. I didn't worry about punctuation and I didn't try to analyze my thoughts. My ill-trained counselor would have wanted to take over and protect me with an over analysis and poorly timed conclusion. Instead, I just wrote. Sometimes, writing took the format of bullet points and other times, sentences.

Challenge:

As cathartic as charting was, reading what I wrote was equally important.

Depending on the situation, I would read what I had charted the day before. Sometimes, if I had journaled during lunch, I needed to read and decompress that night when I got home. There was no real rhyme or reason for the times that I would review what I wrote. I was more concerned with how I felt when I began to review my writing. I needed to be in a mental space where I was calm and able to digest what I had written. Sometimes, depending on the level of stress, this would require soft instrumental music, calm lighting, aromatherapy, and prayer before I even reviewed my writing.

As I began to review my writing, one thing was very important to me. I had to be able to separate the objective from the subjective. In other words, the facts from the opinions or assumptions. To do this, I asked myself if others were in the area during these occurrences, what aspects of the story would we all agree on? These, of course, are the facts. Then, I asked what aspects of the story we could potentially disagree on? These were the assumptions or opinions. I want to be clear, I (and you do too) have a right to feelings based on experiences. This activity was in no way used to negate that. However, I was able to challenge my own perceptions of my supervisor's behavior, my behavior, outside influences, ineffective organizational systems, being stuck or feeling hopeless.

Challenging and reflection helped me to minimize the things that were insignificant and focus on the things that were impactful. I discovered, after being in an unhealthy working environment for so long, even small things were magnified. Charting (or journaling) provided me with an unfiltered outlet to pour my feelings, experiences, behaviors, and reactions into. Challenging helped me to take that raw emotion, put it in perspective, and break it down into actionable interventions. Once I accomplished this, I was able to critically think and strategize. During this time of charting and challenging, my workplace situation remained the same. Neither my supervisor or my organizational structure changed. But, in spite of that, I was finding my peace and equally important, I was reclaiming my health.

Change:

Consistent with not being able to un-see truth once you really see it, challenging perceptions led to the development of action steps. If I found that my behavior or reaction was inconsistent with what my personal value system was, I made a plan of action of how I would try to react the next time. In managing expectations of myself, if I did not successfully implement my plan of action in the next scenario, I gave myself grace. Instead of cloaking myself in feelings of disappointment, I charted and challenged again. Unknowingly to me at the time, my inner counselor was being trained and started to get more in sync with my actual emotions. When stressed, I began to practice mindful breathing and focus on just being instead of feeling forced to react or ignore.

Okay, this is where it may get hard for some of us. I know I struggled with it...understanding how hard behavior change was for me, I worked hard to extend that same grace to my supervisor. Nope, it wasn't easy. As awful as it sounds, I kind of enjoyed simplifying her behavior by blaming it on an anatomical defect related to the size of her heart. This characterization only helped me to justify my response to her. It did little to help me find my own personal peace and health in the situation.

Another action step that I took was to take breaks when necessary. Initially, when I started, I concluded that taking breaks was either going to be forced due to my physical symptoms or by choice. I know that time off may not appear to be a viable option for everyone. You will have to be the best judge of where you are and how your physical and mental health is being impacted. Sometimes, a break will come in the form of time off and other times it may be simply going to the bathroom to collect yourself.

Before I started my journey to heal, I took breaks. However, they often came at the point where I was so stressed that I was almost incapacitated with little to no energy to relax and decompress while off. The day before it was time for me to return, I would get headaches and sick to the stomach. Now, my breaks were scheduled and more strategically planned. Charting and challenging helped me to see just how much of my precious time, outside of work, that I was allowing this circumstance to consume.

I guess you could say that there may be a fourth "C" and if so, it would be to choose. However, I've decided not to list it as a standalone because charting, challenging, and changing will inherently lead to choosing. Barring any direct physical abuse or harassment (i.e., sexual harassment), the need to stay or go is a decision for you and perhaps your loved ones alone to make. You have to do what is best for your professional growth and development, your financial outlook, and more importantly your mental peace and physical health. However, whatever option that you chose, know that consistent peace will come from within. Getting a new supervisor, changing careers, or a systematic organizational shake-up may or may not solve the problem. True and consistent peace will come from within. ☐

One Last Story

Before we wrap up, I want to share one last story with you. Although I don't know him personally, I read a story about an extremely talented young man who was selected for a new position. While this seems positive, the problem was that the position he was selected for was already occupied by an influential executive. To make matters worse, the executive had no intentions of leaving and felt that his identity was intimately tied to his authority and position of influence. Due to the executive's own personal insecurities and shortcomings, he suffered a mental breakdown. His behavior became so erratic that others around him noticed it. In an odd turn of events, the executive recruited the new young talent to help out and relieve some of his stress. Of course, the executive did not know that the young talent had actually been selected as his replacement.

In many cases, this would have been all the ammunition that some of us would have needed to send for security and a cardboard box to help the executive find a way to manage his stress in another environment. However, in this story, the young talent performed his job with humility, deference to the executive, and a spirit of excellence. It is a situation that is hard to imagine. Some of us may have strong suspicions that our boss has mental issues, but this young talent knew what his boss was dealing with. He often saw the executive having full meltdowns and was the only person who could calm the executive down. As the young talent excelled in his work, instead of the executive being grateful, he became jealous and plotted the young man's demise. Talk about an unhealthy working environment!

If this story sounds familiar, it is because it is the Bible story of Saul and David. Saul was the reigning king of Israel, whose disobedience caused him to be rejected by God. In a secret ceremony with David and his family, a prophet communicated God's decision to choose David as the new king. David was not looking to take Saul's job and had nothing to do with Saul's job being taken away. Nevertheless, the better David performed his job, the more Saul hated him.

I share this story because unlike my story, David's approach to working in an unsafe unhealthy working environment was beyond reproach. To save his life, David ended up running away. Even when he returned, he behaved with a spirit of humility. I want you to understand that it is possible that you may do everything that is within your abilities to remain humble and excel in your work. That does not mean your situation is going to change. It could mean that you have outgrown the current position that you are in and you are called to something greater. Although David was challenged in ways beyond our understanding, the prophet was clear about David's future. At this point, you may not have that level of clarity. However, it is possible that nothing you do in your current environment will lead you to contentment. I encourage you to read David's story. Can you see ways that he charted (how about those psalms), challenged, and changed?

As you read this book, I am honored that you allowed me to go on this journey with you. Wherever you are in your path, I pray that this book has helped you to find peace in any workplace situation.

From Toxic to Tranquility:
How to claim your peace in a toxic work
environment